MUSIC CDS BY GREG TAMBLYN

The Shootout At The I'm OK,
You're OK Corral

Greg Tamblyn, NCW:
No Credentials Whatsoever

How Could Life Be
Better Than This

Art From The Heart

The Grand Design

Saving The World From
Whiny Victim Love Songs

For song samples and order details go to:

www.gregtamblyn.com

"Fasten your seatbelt! This troubadour takes you on a series of unforgettable adventures that warm your heart and tickle your funny bone. Greg weaves a good story, and his vocabulary has really improved since college. Happy trails in Greg's Universe."

~ *Brian Luke Seaward, PhD*, author of *Stand Like Mountain, Flow Like Water* and *Stressed Is Desserts Spelled Backward*.

"Greg Tamblyn's songs have always made my soul feel warm and comfy. Now he has a book to do the same thing. I love how he combines travel in the world with travel of a spiritual sort, and I'm grateful he let me come along."

~ *Victoria Moran*, author of *Creating a Charmed Life*

"With wisdom, humor, and a warm heart, Greg Tamblyn brings refreshing perspectives to the chance adventures of everyday life."

~ *Peter Russell*, author of *The Global Brain*, and *From Science to God*

"Life may or may not be a terminal condition, but laughter goes on forever. Let's take a joyride into the profound and the absurd, the weird and the whimsical, the sacred and the silly. Sooner or later you find out these are all the same thing."

~ *Greg Tamblyn, NCW (No Credentials Whatsoever)*

ATILLA
THE GATE AGENT
Travel Tales and Life Lessons
From a Musical Laf-ologist
by

Greg Tamblyn

www.gregtamblyn.com

Published by TuneTown Records
P. O. Box 45258
Kansas City, MO 64171-8258

ISBN 978-0-9792348-1-1

US $11.95

THANKS!

In no particular order, to...

All you brave readers and travelers who invested the time and money to let me share my musings with you, in these pages and in my songs

Also those of you who have accompanied me on some of these adventures

All my newsletter subscribers who suggested this piece of fine literature (hopefully you're now going to actually buy it...)

All the people and characters who let me write about them, whether they knew it or not

Rebecca Price (RebeccaPrice.com) for excellent book design services

Kathleen Smith (LeaderScore.com) for proofreading and loads of other help.

Rosalind Sedacca (ChildCenteredDivorce.com) for proofreading, and marketing

Dr. Carol Cole (DrCarolCole.com) for her suggestion to add song lyrics

Author G. Roger Corey for suggesting Parts I and II, proofreading, and editing

Claudia Corey for feedback, suggestions

Jeff Tamblyn (UnconditionalFilms.com) for feedback, suggestions

Jamie Rich (OpenCircleOnline.com) for feedback, suggestions

John Schuster (SKAlliance.com) for encouragement, feedback

Thanks, continued...

Carol Hansen Grey (CarolHansenGrey.com) for proof-reading, suggestions

Victor Grey (CustomDynamic.net) for proofreading, suggestions

The Sheafor clan and friends for feedback

Marilyn Hager and Andrew Adelman (PurpleFishMedia.com) for web design

Richard Helm of Nashville, TN for songwriting and a ton of encouragement

Laura Baker (Author-Coach.com) for advice

Richard Crane (RCraneLaw.com) and Eileen Tremblay for time to write on the boat

Mom for making me go to school and learn to read and write, sort of

Authors Larry Dossey (DosseyDossey.com), Luke Seaward (BrianLukeSeaward.net), Bowen White (BowenWhite.com), Pam Grout (PamGrout.com), Victoria Moran (VictoriaMoran.com), Mardy Grothe (Chiasmus.com), Peter Russel (PeterRussell.com) for their fine and only marginally coerced endorsements

Sophia Tamblyn for cover photography

Chris Dennis Photography, Kansas City, front cover head shot

Matt Nichols Photography, Kansas City, back cover head shot

David Roth of DavidRothMusic.com for submitting to a cartoon drawing with me

The unknown artist at Universal Studios for the actual cartoon

CONTENTS

PART ONE ~ OUTER TRAVEL

1. Read This First .... page   13
2. Exotic Kansas................................... page   15
3. They Say It Never Rains In
    Southern Zihuatanejo .... page 19
4. Life And Change In One Man's
    China................................... page   21
5. Atilla The Gate Agent................................... page   25
6. Only In Alaska: The Tractor
    The Piano, And The River .... page   31
7. Bog Snorkelling In Ireland .... page   35
8. Girl On A Plane................................... page   39
9. Chairman Mao's Lighter................................... page   41
10. Monkey Business................................... page   47
11. The Full Monty At The Airport................... page   51
12. Chop Suey, Y'all................................... page   53
13. Rock Star Waxes Poetic .... page   55
14. Stand Like Mountain,
    Move Like Water................................... page   57
15. Ou'est la Salle de Bain?
    (Where Is The Bathroom?)...........................page   63
16. The Sewers Of Paris .... page   65

17.   My Inner Wimp Meets The
      Inca Trail.. page 67

18.   The Dangers Of Networking....................... page 71

19.   Out Front In The Outback.............................page 75

PART TWO ~ INNER TRAVEL

20.   Saving The World From Whiny
      Victim Love Songs...page 81

21.   Six Months To Live: The Story
      Of Evy McDonald ....page 85

22.   Patch Adams: Clown To The World............page 91

23.   Dad Finally Gets An Ace ....page 95

      About the author..page 99

PART ONE

Outer Travel

"If there's anything more important than my ego around, I want it caught and shot now." ~ *Douglas Adams,*
The Hitchhiker's Guide to the Galaxy

Chapter 1

READ THIS FIRST

I once had an engagement in the town of Normal, Illinois. I was delighted to learn that a place called Normal actually existed, because I happen to live just a few miles from the town of Peculiar, Missouri. I don't think it's any accident of the universe that I'm a lot closer to Peculiar than Normal.

A few years ago, I started writing short newsletters to keep in contact with people who had come to my concerts and were either brave or foolish enough to give me their addresses. I had no idea then how much I was going to enjoy this little chore. Eventually, enough people suggested they would make a good book that I decided to humor them. So here it is.

These stories are mostly about people and events I've bumped into in the course of getting away with writing songs, making music, and having fun with people for a living. I don't think there's any particular theme, but if you find one, let me know and I'll give you credit.

There is some learning here, however. Definitely for me, and hopefully even for you. I've been blessed to meet some interesting people and see some fascinating places. Frequently these have been "growth opportunities," and sometimes even springboards for songs, as the occasional included lyrics will attest. My sincere desire is that you'll be entertained, and maybe even think and feel a little differently in the process.

Happy travels,

Greg Tamblyn
Kansas City
September 2006

"A good traveler has no fixed plans."
~ Lao Tzu, Tao Te Ching

Chapter 2

EXOTIC KANSAS

I boarded a flight home from San Francisco to Kansas City and found a real party going on back in coach. Everybody seemed to know each other and they were all roaming around the cabin, laughing, talking, and generally having a great time. It turned out they were mostly pharmaceutical reps from the west coast on their way to K.C. for a convention. I remember thinking there must have been a lot of free samples being passed around.

I was trapped in a middle seat, and after an hour in the midst of the frivolity I was feeling like the token nerd at a fraternity party. Then the woman next to me, still relatively sober at this point, turned and made an astute observation. She said, "You're not part of this group, are you?"

I told her no, and she asked, "So why are you going to Kansas City?"

I said, "Well, I live there."

"Really!" she exclaimed, and her eyes opened wide. "You know, I grew up in New York City and I've lived my whole adult life in San Francisco, and when I think about somebody living in Kansas, it just sounds painful to me."

Painful. That was the word she used.

I've noticed we Kansans get this a lot. In the movie Dr. No, for example, Dr. No tells James Bond, "The satellite is at present over Kansas. Well, if we destroy Kansas the world may not hear about it for years."

People just don't seem to link up Kansas with the word "exotic." But that's because they just don't know. They haven't been there.

Twenty years or so ago, when I was still singing in bars and hotels, I got hired to do sort of a Holiday Inn circuit around Kansas. I played in places like Great Bend, Hutchinson, Hayes, Salina, Dodge City, and Wichita. I got to see Kansas the way few people do: up close and personal. And I discovered Kansas has stuff that's just as cool and exotic as anywhere else, if you know where to look.

For example, over in Cawker City, we have the World's Largest Ball of Twine. And it's still growing. As of this writing it's more than 12 ft in diameter and weighs as much as several elephants (17,801 lbs). That amounts to more than seven million feet of twine. It's enough to stretch from Cawker City to the Ripley's Believe-It-Or-Not Museums in Orlando, San Antonio, or San Francisco.

But that's not all. Back east a little bit in Abilene (home of some guy named Dwight Eisenhower), we have the Museum of Independent Telephony. Now, I know a lot of you have been wondering if there even *was* a museum of independent telephony, and if so, where it might be. Well, good news: it's right here in Kansas.

Southwest of there in Greensburg is the World's Deepest Hand Dug Well. Maybe you can't see it from space like the Great Wall, but still, some cowboys dug a long time on that thing. Over a year, in fact. It's 109 feet deep and 32 feet wide, and sits just a stone's throw away from the World's Fourth-Largest Pallasite Meteorite. (1,000 lbs.)

For all you agricultural types, over in LaCrosse we have the one and only Barbed Wire Museum. My guess is that most of you probably didn't even know there was more than one kind of barbed wire. Well guess what? There are over 2,000. See, you just learned something. And you haven't even been there yet.

In Lucas, Kansas, there is — honest to God — a sculpture of the Garden of Eden which takes up an entire acre. Not only that, it's made totally and completely, 100% out of cement. 2,273 bags to be exact. Nowhere else in the world can you see that. Only in Kansas.

There's also a wonderful attraction out west in Oakley called Prairie Dog Town, "Home of the Giant Prairie Dog." According to the brochure, you can "See Animals Not In The Zoo, and Many More!" (Okay, so maybe we're not great copywriters in Kansas, but we have neat stuff.)

But truth be told, the best place I found in all this roaming around was just across the state line outside Clinton, Missouri.

It's called "Larry's Lawn Ornaments and Cheese Shop."

You have to admit, it takes a rare kind of genius to find two things that go together as well as lawn ornaments and cheese.

"Hey, that's a great little birdbath you picked out there. How about a nice sharp cheddar to go with it!"

See, with the right attitude you can have fun just about anywhere. Even in Kansas.

"The really happy person is one who can enjoy the scenery when on a detour." ~ *Unknown*

Chapter 3

THEY SAY IT NEVER RAINS IN SOUTHERN ZIHUATANEJO

The main bus station in Zihuatanejo, Mexico, is an unusual collision of man and nature. It's about the size of a football field, with a 50 to 60 foot high ceiling. It also happens to be a giant, unintentional aviary.

As I waited early in the morning for the bus to Acapulco (which never showed up), I became aware of what sounded like a very large number of birds. Thinking this odd, I looked up in amazement to the sight of hundreds, maybe even thousands of birds in the rafters, mostly sitting, a few flying around. My first thought was, *Shades of Alfred Hitchcock.... how the bleep did they get in here?* Then I noticed the building had been designed with several feet of space between the walls and the roof, interrupted by only occasional supports, giving the birds easy access in and out.

As I sat there taking all this in, a question began to form in my mind, having to do with bird poop. Like where exactly do all these birds do their business? So I swung my gaze down to the marble floor, and sure enough it was *covered* with bird droppings! (A fact I hadn't noticed upon entering because it was 6:30 AM, a time when I'm normally still a few hours from waking consciousness. And also because I was anxious to get to the counter and get my ticket. For the bus to Acapulco. Which never showed up.)

As I began to pay more attention to this phenomenon, I noticed I could actually hear the rhythmic splats of bird poop hitting the floor, approximately every five seconds or so. Feeling some concern about the appearance and hygiene of things like my hair, clothes, and luggage, I immediately and gratefully ascertained that, at least for the moment, neither I nor my luggage was parked directly beneath any member of this enormous flock

My relief was short-lived, however, when a few minutes later something spooked the birds and they all became simultaneously agitated, suddenly flying around crazily and noisily like water molecules that just hit 212 degrees. At that moment the splats got much louder and more frequent, and it was quite literally raining bird do-do.

Just then, in the midst of this bizarre storm, something landed on my lap.

No, not bird poop. A feather. I took this to be a sign of divine protection, because somehow, miraculously, I was unscathed.

About that time I looked around and noticed one other interesting fact: I was the only person actually sitting inside the bus station. Everyone else was either outside or standing in the doorways. Most of them were looking at me, with an expression that seemed to say, "stupid gringo." This struck me as a beautiful example of the term "local knowledge."

Suddenly I felt a strong urge to move. And to buy an umbrella.

So the next time the bus doesn't show, look around. You might see something you've never seen before.

"If you tell the truth you don't have to remember anything." ~ Mark Twain

Chapter 4

LIFE AND CHANGE IN ONE MAN'S CHINA

The Russians have a saying about the difference between communism and capitalism: "In communism, man exploits man. In capitalism, the reverse is true."

When Li was four years old in China, he watched his father being tortured. This was 1970, and the torturers were the Red Guard of Mao's Cultural Revolution. It was a hot summer day. They made his father put on a fur hat, fur coat, fur pants, and then semi-squat in the middle of a ring of small clay ovens. The ovens were hot with burning coal. If his father squatted too low, he would get too close to the ovens, maybe catch on fire. If he stood up, the Red Guards would beat him on the head, maybe knock him unconscious. This went on for a whole day. Then more days. Then a few months altogether.

The Red Guard wanted him to admit he was a spy. He had left the army a few years before. They figured there must be something wrong for him to quit the army — such a good position — so he must be a spy. Li's father knew that if he admitted spying (not true), the torture would end. But then he would get thrown into a prison, and most likely disappear. A lot of people disappeared then. Millions, in fact. His father was a strong man, strong enough to withstand this torture, and smart enough not to say anything. So he survived.

Li watched this when he was four years old, and remembered.

The strange thing is that the Communist party propaganda was so persuasive and pervasive, that just a few years later as an adolescent Li was seriously considering joining. But somehow, every time he was about to sign up, something inside kept him from being able to fully commit. Probably the memory of seeing his father squatting inside that ring of ovens.

So instead of the Party, Li poured his passion into school, and did exceptionally well. He was one of only three students from his entire province allowed to go to Beijing and study English. Soon came another life changing event.

As Li's education progressed, he became more politically idealistic, and grew disillusioned with the corruption and degeneration in the Party. So in the spring of 1989 it was natural for him to join the student movement in Tiananmen Square, which he did enthusiastically. It was a heady time, with growing masses of students swelling the square daily. They were joined by workers and even professionals, all of whom were fed up with the system and wanted a change to democracy, the sooner the better.

Li could tell the Chinese people were behind them. Everyone he talked to was supportive, enthusiastic, ready for change. Li often slept at the square. On the occasions he and his friends slept at school, taxi drivers would not charge them for rides back to the square to demonstrate. Food, toilets, and other necessities almost magically appeared for the demonstrators.

Then one evening in late May, as the demonstration was in full force, Li and some friends stopped a truckload of soldiers headed for the square. They explained to these young soldiers why students were demonstrating so passionately. They told the soldiers that corruption and degeneration were the reasons their military pay was so pitifully low. They explained how nepotism was rife throughout the party and the government.

Li could tell the young soldiers believed them. He swears he even saw tears on their faces. He knows they were getting through to them.

This is the last thing he remembers until he woke up in the hospital. His head was throbbing with pain, and he later found out he had been hit from behind by a policeman. Li was in the hospital with a concussion for seven days. When he was well enough to leave he was sent back to his remote province.

He never found out what happened to the seven friends who were with him. They disappeared.

Many months later, Li was allowed to return to Beijing and finish his studies. For weeks he was subjected to surprise interrogations by police at odd hours. These would sometimes last all night. Like his father 20 years before, he knew enough to say very little. Like most people, he felt the students had been defeated.

But according to Li, in 1992 the Chinese leader Deng Xiaoping realized it had been a mistake to kill the students in Tiananmen Square three years before. Deng then went to the south of China for a month to live with farmers and factory workers. After this, he announced a new policy of privatization of some businesses, and partnership with the government of some others. This was actually the slow beginning of a radical change for China.

Li feels that in many ways this policy has been hugely successful. The Chinese people enjoy more freedom now than they have in decades. Li could now travel to the US or almost anywhere else if he chooses. Despite high unemployment in places, problems with farm policies, and a widening gulf between haves and have-nots, Li claims the Chinese economy is arguably the most stable in Asia.

Li has softened his idealistic stance. He feels now that it is not possible to change a huge monolithic structure like the Chinese Communist party, or the Chinese government, overnight. He is more practical, more realistic, and more patient. He has a wife and young son now, and is more focused on the responsibilities — and pleasures — of everyday life. He knows that more change will come, but that it will take time. The young people of China today are interested in progress. They have access to the internet. They want the freedom and prosperity they see in the rest of the free world. They have no interest in the politics and the ideas of Mao. This will bring change.

For these reasons, Li now views Deng Xiaoping as a liberator of China. Deng was, in Li's words, "a smart guy." And because of this, he sees the student movement of 1989 as an unqualified success.

The policy of China now is "One country, two systems." Communism and capitalism.

"Without music, life would be a mistake." ~ Nietzsche

Chapter 5

ATILLA THE GATE AGENT

For a year or so I had been thinking that as much as I loved my old Takamine maple-finish acoustic-electric six string guitar (affectionately known as Bubbles the Blonde), and even though this guitar had been my steady companion for ten years, maybe it was time to upgrade to a better instrument. Something that sounded better, and also was a better finger-picking guitar. But the idea of hitting the guitar shops for a big long search was somewhat daunting to me, both from a time standpoint, and also from a money standpoint. Good guitars are expensive.

Another challenge was that guitar stores are frequently staffed by a demographic group we could label "Young Rock Musicians." This is no knock against young rock musicians, because I used to be one. But see if in your mind these two things go together: *Young Rock Musicians* and *Great Customer Service*. Kind of a disconnect, isn't it? Most of the time anyway.

So I put off making any kind of decision or even looking, and just kept it on the back burner. Sort of in the Need-To-But-Don't-Want-To category.

That is until fate intervened at the Honolulu airport in the form of a woman I will affectionately refer to as Atilla the Gate Agent. For some reason — power trip? bad lunch? — Atilla absolutely refused to let me carry my guitar on the plane, as I had been doing every week for years with no problem. All my attempts at sincere, friendly, win-win negotiation (and finally even begging) were curtly rebuffed. So reluctantly I surrendered it to her in its soft case — a lightly padded case with no real protection. I asked her to please let the baggage people know it was fragile and unprotected. Without a nod or a smile, Atilla took it, gate checked it, and I prayed for the best.

But when we got to San Francisco my guitar was in an altered state. One commonly known as "splinters." It was like a souvenir from a Who concert. It was not going to be played again, except maybe as a percussion instrument.

Needless to say, for me this was a stressful event. Especially considering I had two gigs there in the next couple of days. My thoughts and feelings toward Atilla were not something I could share with you outside of group therapy. Especially knowing there had been plenty of room on the plane, and essentially no good reason for the forced gate check.

Enter three angels in the form of flight attendants, who felt terrible about this horrible injustice, marched me down to baggage service, and saw to it that the manager there understood that this had been wrong and unnecessary, and that it would be extremely right and proper for her to do something to make things all better. The manager, however, let me know that company policy strictly dictated they never took responsibility for damage to musical instruments. If I wanted to, I could come back in the morning and talk to a higher manager, but the policy was firm.

So after a sleepless night of unsuccessfully trying not to be furious with Atilla, and feeling exhausted from my anger, I returned the next morning to speak with the higher manager. All the way to the airport I was asking silently for help (just to keep my cool) from an even higher power.

And it worked! I was calm. After hearing my story, the higher manager left to confer with an even supremely higher manager. When they came back, they reminded me about their company policy of no compensation. I said I knew about that. But then to my great surprise, relief, joy, happiness, and improved digestion, they said they had decided to buy me a new guitar. I thanked them sincerely and got out of there before they could change their minds.

Since I was in San Francisco, I asked my musician friends where to go. They told me the Haight-Ashbury Music Center was the only real place to go for a serious musician. (Evidently they didn't know me as well as I thought.) Anyway, I had the pleasure of spending the next two days in Haight-Ashbury. In case you haven't been there lately, it's kind of like a corner of the Twilight Zone where the '60s coexists along with the present day and some future decade I can't even imagine. There is every conceivable kind of hairdo, tattoo, pierced body part, alternative clothing, spiritual orientation, and dietary preference. I was definitely not in Kan-

-sas anymore. Not even in Peculiar, Missouri. It was an experiential journey through the senses.

I also got to try out a few dozen guitars in the store, and the sales people were not only friendly but incredibly helpful. They were patient, knowledgeable, and willing to answer my endless questions. The whole experience turned out to be one of the more entertaining and colorful of the year.

But the main thing is, I ended up with this great new guitar I'm absolutely crazy about! I love it so much, I haven't missed the old one for ten seconds. It's a much better instrument than my old guitar, more fun to play, and even sounds better. It's hundreds of dollars more expensive than my old guitar, and it was totally paid for by the airline!

And the thing is, I owe it all to Atilla the Gate Agent.

You just never know who's going to turn out to be an angel in your life. They might not look like it.

I THOUGHT I WOULD MISS HER
(Greg Tamblyn)

I thought I would miss her, the last time I kissed her
The last time I kissed her goodbye
She'd been a good friend and there at the end
It was all I could do not to cry

She had a face that was not commonplace
She was elegant, simple, and fun
Her voice was so lovely, could melt me like putty
She'd always been my only one

They said at the airport it's a full flight and therefore
She could not ride with me on the plane
I hoped it wouldn't matter but she was just shattered
After that she was never the same

I thought I would miss her
The last time I kissed her
We'd been together so long
But time has a way
Each dawning day
Of moving us surely along

Man I was hurtin', so I started searchin'
To find a new love for myself
But you gotta go slow, it takes time to know
You can't pick one right off the shelf

Does she look really sweet, can she deliver the heat
Does she sing like a bird in your arms
Is she not too high strung, please God, not too young
Have subtle attractions and charms

Yes I thought I would miss her
The last time I kissed her

We'd been together so long
I was in love
But maybe not quite enough
And fate was at work all along

I must admit it happened so quick
It might have been love at first sight
It was such a surprise, when new love
caught my eyes
But I knew for sure after one night

At first I was mad, cursed that airline so bad
For breaking my angel in two
I thought I would miss her, but her little sister
Has stolen my heart through and through

And I thought I would miss her
The last time I kissed her
But just like a gift from afar
Time has a way
Each dawning day
And I'm in love with my new guitar

"Since everything is none other than exactly as it is,
one may well just break out in laughter."
~ *Long Chen Pa*

Chapter 6

ONLY IN ALASKA....THE TRACTOR, THE PIANO, AND THE RIVER
(How I Spent My Summer Vacation)

Alaska has always been something of a fantasy land to me, with images of bears, eagles, moose, tall mountains, and colorful, oddball people like the characters on Northern Exposure. When I finally got there, what I found really wasn't too far from that.

I was reunited with a college roommate named Kit I hadn't seen in over 20 years. His brothers' names are Carson, Custer, and Brett Maverick. (I'm not kidding.) Kit lives in Anchorage, in a regular house right in the suburbs. He also has a 1500 acre homestead out in the wilderness, a couple of hours north of town. My first full day in Alaska, he drove me up there and said we were going to float a player piano down the river from the homestead to another guy's truck. I asked him why, and Kit said because the other guy wanted it.

Thinking that the average player piano probably weighs as much as a small elephant, I asked how we were going to do this. Kit said we'd figure it out.

The piano-floating crew turned out to be Kit, myself, and a couple of other guys, one of whom —Elmo — was inheriting the piano. Elmo is a very energetic, white-haired, crewcut guy in his late 60s who smiles a lot, talks a lot, and looks like he's worked hard every day of his life. I have no doubt he could outwork me all day long. I think he plays pretty hard too, because about once an hour he asked us if we wanted some beer or whiskey.

When we got to the boat ramp, Kit and Larry got their hip waders on, launched the little boat, and we motored down the Susitna River a few miles. Arriving at the homestead, I was mildly awestruck not only at the size and beauty of the place, but also at seeing almost every kind of heavy equipment known to man. Kit's dad, Wally, who founded the homestead back in the '60s, was the kind of bigger than life guy who liked to do everything himself. He bought everything from tree-pullers to earth movers, his own sawmill, and even an enormous pickup truck on tank-type tracks that can maneuver through five feet of swamp. I asked Kit why we didn't just move the piano on the aforementioned tank-truck, and Kit said because it would take a couple of days and a couple of hundred dollars worth of gas. The old homestead is pretty far out in the sticks. There are no roads to the place.

After a tour of several cabins and an impressive log home filled with Remington cowboy sculptures (something tells me it was Wally who named all the boys), as well as a beautiful view of the river and Mt. McKinley, we came to a giant tractor with a huge forklift on the front, containing the aforementioned player piano. Kit, who drives all these giant machines around like they were Honda Civics, climbed up into the seat, steered the tractor a few hundred yards down to the river, lowered the forklift, and the real engineering began.

In the end, we did it Elmo's way. We slid the piano off the forklift and onto some timbers, and then down the timbers onto the back of what seemed to me our very small (for the purpose) 18-foot open riverboat. Amazingly to me, nobody's fingers got smashed, nobody's feet got crushed, and the piano didn't slide into the river.

Then it started raining.

Elmo found a tarp, got the piano covered up, and asked us if we wanted some whiskey. We said no, Kit let me drive the tractor back to the shed, and Jack, the fourth guy, filleted the four large salmon we had caught in less than an hour (sort of as an after-thought). One for each of us.

Then it was off down the river in the rain with a big piano on the back of a little boat. Elmo stood on the back of the boat drinking a beer and making sure the piano didn't slide off into the river. We got to the boat ramp, loaded the fully loaded boat onto the boat trailer, and slowly pulled it up the ramp to Larry's truck. Elmo offered us a beer, we said not just now, and proceeded to figure out how to get the piano from the boat onto Elmo's pickup.

It turned out to be another board-sliding operation that came off relatively smoothly.

That's what really impressed me about the whole thing. For a crazy, seat of the pants type operation, these guys made it seem easy. We got the piano to Elmo's house, unloaded it, said no thanks to some whiskey, and toured Elmo's collection of 35 snowmobiles from the 1960s, some of which actually work.

Then we drove back to Kit's home in the suburbs, where a moose was in his front yard eating a tree. Kit threw basketballs at it to shoo it away while I laughed.

*"May you have warm words on a cold evening,
a full moon on a dark night, and the road downhill all the
way to your door." ~ An Irish blessing*

Chapter 7

BOG SNORKELLING IN IRELAND

You know you've had a great trip when you stumble onto something so weird and different, so out of your conceptual comfort zone that it sticks in your mind like dog hair on a wool suit. And when it involves two words you never in your most inspired or inebriated moments dreamed would ever go together, it's even better.

For me, in Ireland, it was Bog Snorkelling.

The first time I heard it I was hooked, even though I didn't have a clue what it was. (I did, however, think it was a great name for a rock band.) It conjured up images so wild and dark, I could barely contain my glee. I had to find out more.

We had just climbed up and down 670 ancient stone steps without any handrails in a driving rain and blustery winds on a steep, rocky moonscape of an island known as Skellig Michael. It's ten miles out into the rough Atlantic from the safe, cozy Irish coastline. Back in the sixth century some Irish monks hatched the rather bizarre notion that it would be a good and Holy thing to row out to this giant, jagged, jutting hunk of rock, somehow climb to the windy top (this would have been before the stone steps, because they built them), and erect some stone huts. Then they would live up there without any material comforts as a sacrifice to God. (Learning this, you get the feeling that the Irish beer must have been freely available even back then.)

So they did it, and for several centuries this was The Place To Pilgrimage for your basic Irish ascetic. And if it wasn't stark and forbidding enough, you could always crawl 12 feet or so out onto a narrow, plank-like rock promontory and kiss the base of a cross that stood 700 feet above the jagged rocks and sea below.

It's an unforgettable place to visit, and as this was something of an adventure tour of Ireland, I was eager to see what was next.

So Dave and Mark (our highly competent Vagabond Adventure Tour guides) mentioned that they wanted to take us out to jump on the Irish bog. I jokingly asked if bog-jumping is one of the ancient Gaelic sports played only in Ireland, like hurling. Now the phrase "bog snorkelling" may make you feel like hurling, but that's not what Irish hurling is. I can say this with certainty, because we watched the All-Ireland Hurling Finals between Cork and Galway. Cork won, for all of you holding your breath.

Hurling is one of those field sports like soccer, football, or rugby, where one team tries to get the ball into the goal more times than the other team. Except that in hurling the men have wooden bats ("hurls") to hit the ball viciously through the air while running at full speed without any padding or evidently much in the way of a self-preservation instinct. My lasting impression was that it looked like the best way I have ever seen to lose a few teeth. Or possibly an ear.

Even so, it's a terribly exciting sport. We all got really involved in pulling for Galway, since we were watching it in the actual County Galway itself, inside a lovely little pub surrounded by dozens of highly excited Galwegians with their few hundred pints of Guinness. Also since the event has roughly the same level of sporting significance as the Super Bowl does in the States.

Anyway, Dave replied that no, there's no sport of Bog Jumping. But there is the sport of Bog Snorkelling, and to understand it, we had to experience the bog. For all the non-geologists in the group, Dave and Mark explained that the bog is simply the remains of ancient plants and animals compressed into layers. It's basically very young coal. And for millennia the Irish have been cutting the bog into bricks, drying it, and burning it for fuel. Some of them even say they like the smell. I suspect that's after a few pints.

Now the bog is not like any ground you have ever walked on. It's spongy and soft, and reminds me of a giant, gentle trampoline. Dave told half the group to jump up and down together, and the rest of us felt the earth move and shake, like that Carole King song. It was weird, but fun.

Then we took turns cutting bricks out of the bog so we could see how soft it was. But what you easily discern is that cutting the bog creates long channels about the width of a swimming lane, and they tend to fill up with an oozing, dark, murky, unimaginably dank, soupy substance that surely contains everything scary and horrible from all the ancient Celtic myths and legends. Beowulf and Grindel are probably down there somewhere. Mark told us to be very careful not to fall in it, because you could quite easily just sink out of sight. I presume what he meant was sink right into the nether world of demons and bog monsters. He looked serious, and I believed him.

Somewhere, somehow (probably in a pub after a hurling final), somebody got the idea that it would be a fun and reasonable thing to strap on a snorkel and swim through this stuff. And even make it a competition.

This is evidently not without precedent. In very ancient Irish culture (so we were told by our highly competent tour guides, who could have been making this up) one of the ways you proved you were man enough to be king was to first parade naked before the tribe to demonstrate your manliness, then bathe in a giant cauldron of soup made of horse parts from a mare that had been sacrificed for this purpose. (I think there was also some sex with the mare involved, although our guides were not specific on this point.) The king and tribe would then drink the soup of horse parts, and presumably whatever had been under the king's toenails, to absorb the power of the animal.

So Bog Snorkelling is really just the latest incarnation of the ancient Celtic or even Neolithic way of confronting the scary, dark side of the unconscious and the creepy. There is a competition and timing aspect to it, but even if you don't win the race, just getting in the slimy bog pool and snorkeling 50-60 feet would say a lot about your courage. Or sanity. Or sobriety.

The only disappointing thing about it all was finding out that wetsuits and swim masks are allowed. I'm sure they would have been sneered at by the ancient Celtic kings. Maybe there is a sanitation factor or something to consider nowadays, but the truth is we're probably just not as rugged as the Bog Lords of Olde. (Another good name for a band.)

Okay, I know what you're thinking: So how was it? Well, honesty compels me to admit I didn't actually try it. But not from lack of desire.

Our highly competent adventure tour guides, not imagining for a moment that anyone from the States would be crazy enough to consider doing this, did not actually have the required snorkelage equipment on hand. This is an oversight I'm sure they'll correct for the next group.

And besides, I need a noble purpose to take me back to Ireland as soon as possible.

Bog Snorkelling takes place in Wales, Ireland and possibly wherever there are bogs. The world championships are in Wales every August. Official website:
http://llanwrtyd-wells.powys.org.uk/bog.html

Vagabond Adventure Tours website:
www.vagabond-ireland.com

"The church says: The body is a sin.
Science says: The body is a machine.
Advertising says: The body is a business.
The Body says: I am a fiesta."
~Eduardo Galeano

Chapter 8

GIRL ON A PLANE

I was squeezed into the window seat of the plane with two wide-bodied guys between me and the aisle. It was definitely going to be a long cramped flight. But after we took off, I glanced over my shoulder and saw to my great joy and relief there were two empty seats in the row behind me. Amazingly, neither of the two large fellows sharing my row seemed motivated to move, so I volunteered.

I had no sooner settled into my roomy new surroundings on the aisle when I noticed that my row-mate, over in the window seat, was an extremely attractive young woman of what appeared to be middle eastern origin. I couldn't help noticing that she was strikingly beautiful — I thought she could be a model. And being a guy who knows a captive audience when he sees one, I started talking to her.

It turns out she was from one of the smaller Arab countries on the Saudi peninsula. Qatar, maybe, but I can't remember for sure. She had grown up in a very strict Muslim household, and had no contact with men all her life, except her brothers. She had always worn a veil in public. Her life was pretty much laid out for her. She would be married to someone of her parents' choosing, she would have babies, and she would live the life her husband wanted her to live. Until then, however, she had been allowed to go to school, and later even college, where she did quite well.

Without telling her family, she applied for a graduate scholarship to a school in Colorado, and unbelievably, got the offer. Emboldened by this success, she somehow was able to cajole her conservative, traditional Muslim father into letting her go to Colorado to study for three years.

So I'm sitting there on the plane looking at this lovely girl in her jean shorts, a tank top, and a lot of very beautiful skin showing, and she tells me she's returning from a vacation with other students in Key West, where they camped on the beach commune-style for two weeks. I'm wondering, Where's the veil? Where's the robe? Where's the Muslim lifestyle?

I comment that she seems to have adapted well to western life. She says yes, within six months of being in America she'd not only dropped the veil, the clothes, and the customs, but she'd moved in with a lover.

Wow, I thought. So what did her parents think of that?

She got a cloudy look on her face and said no no no. They could never know about it. There was no way she could ever tell them. Her father simply would not understand.

But hadn't she been home to see them in these three years?

No, she hadn't. She was afraid of not being able to come back. And even now she was desperately looking for a job so she could get a green card and stay here. The thought of going back to her old life after all this freedom was horrifying.

But how could her family not know? Surely she takes pictures now and then? Doesn't she ever send pictures home to her parents?

Yes, of course she takes pictures. And she sends them home. But she takes two sets. The ones she sends home are the ones with the veils.

"A human being is a part of the whole, called by us "Universe," a part limited in time and space. He experiences himself, his thoughts and feelings as something separated from the rest - a kind of optical delusion of his consciousness. This delusion is a kind of prison for us, restricting us to our personal desires and to affection for a few persons nearest to us. Our task must be to free ourselves from this prison by widening our circle of compassion to embrace all living creatures and the whole of nature in its beauty. Nobody is able to achieve this completely, but the striving for such achievement is in itself a part of the liberation and a foundation for inner security." ~ Albert Einstein, quoted in H Eves Mathematical Circles Adieu

Chapter 9

CHAIRMAN MAO'S LIGHTER

Have you ever had a brilliant gift idea that turned out to be the most embarrassing and humiliating thing you could have brought to the party?

At a conference on consciousness we were told to bring a small, wrapped present to exchange as a means of getting to know each other. The gift was supposed to be related to something significant in our life. After wracking my brains for awhile, and looking around the house, I found the perfect thing: a lighter I had brought back from China. It was a souvenir from the first time I ever hosted a group tour, which has become a yearly event since then.

Ah, but this was no ordinary lighter. It was a solid lighter with some heft to it, covered in bright red enamel. On one side, the imposing face of Chairman Mao stares out at you, totally out of context on this goofy trinket. Sort of like Abraham Lincoln on a box of Wheaties. But the kicker is that when you open the top, it plays a silly (and quite frankly annoying) Chinese marching song, which squeals on and on — lit or not — until you close it.

Or until the battery runs out, should you leave it open for a few days as a sort of Chinese torture for the unlucky people you live with. In short, it's pretty funny. And it kind of reduces Mao to the status of a cartoon, which I like.

I've given a few of these away to friends, and everybody gets a kick out of them. My brother likes to walk down the grocery store aisle with his lighter held aloft, music blaring and people staring. I think he does it to embarrass his daughter. But I digress...

So I felt quite proud of myself for bringing this funny, clever gift that I knew everyone at the conference would find amusing. That first night, all 120 of us were sorted into small circles of eight and instructed to put our presents in the middle. One by one we took turns choosing a gift that someone else had brought, and then we took turns unwrapping them. When someone opened the gift you brought, you explained what meaning it had for you, and in that way we'd get to know a bit about each other.

But what happened in our little circle was a kind of cosmic joke.

Imagine: out of all the 120 people at this event, the one person who ended up with my little wrapped package containing this incredibly funny, brilliantly clever, totally inspired gift of a Chairman Mao lighter, just happened to be the childhood/ life-long friend, as well as the official biographer of.........the Dalai Lama.

I'm not kidding.

He was seated just to my left. I didn't know there would be a Tibetan at this conference. I didn't know there would be a man who, as I later found out, actually fought Chinese soldiers and was forced to flee into exile as they took over and brutalized his country in 1950.

As soon as I saw him pick up the little package, I felt myself shrink about five sizes. What I really wanted was to disappear altogether. If humiliation was a color, I would have been a bright orange smoke bomb, just fizzing away into nothing.

All the time we were going around the circle opening presents, I was sitting there, completely freaked out at the fact that I had brought this insulting gift, and it was going to be unbearably awkward when this gentle, elderly, dignified, much-loved man opened it. Unbelievably embarrassing. Life-shattering buckets of shame. For once in my life, I'd been just a little too clever, and my sick sense of humor had come back to haunt me. How could I possibly explain this to him? What could I say? Especially when all the other were so thoughtful and beautiful. What would he say? What would he do?

When it got to be my turn, I suggested we switch presents.

"Why?" he asked.

"Because I don't think you'll like it. I want you to have something you'll like."

"No," he said. "I want this one."

Slowly and calmly, he unwrapped the lighter. He turned it over, and for a minute just looked at the picture of Mao. I can't remember if he opened the top and played the little song.

After what seemed like forever, during which time I would have gladly traded my whole life to be somewhere else, he spoke.

"Oh," he said firmly. "This is karma."

He looked at me with steady, sincere eyes and said, "This will help me remember to practice compassion."

Postscript
(A letter from a friend at the conference, Alison Sheafor, reporting how Kuno described this experience.)

Dear Greg,

I love that you tell the story about your lighter, but you must tell more of the story. The way you ended it made it sound like he was being polite — but it was MUCH more than that. It was huge, and wonderful.

You should have heard Kuno's talk at the International House after the Conference. He began to talk about his history and connection with the Dalai Lama, and he briefly mentioned his important role as a general in the war. He spoke about how the Chinese killed his parents, family members, and so many of his friends. He talked about his anger at the Chinese — so much anger.

He talked about how the Dalai Lama told him many times, he needed to make peace with the Chinese, to not hate them, to have love in his heart, compassion, forgiveness. He saw no way to do this, it was impossible. He hated them all to such an extent that he wouldn't even eat Chinese food. The Dalai Lama would laugh at this and tell him that Chinese food is very good and his anger is making him miss out on some very good things.

Well, before the conference Kuno was visiting a site of one of the bloody battles between China and Tibet where he lost many friends. He was at the memorial, trying to make peace, but only feeling anger, pain and sadness. He began to cry. A couple was there, crying also. They and Kuno started talking about their losses, and began bonding. After a while they decided to go to a place for some food and to talk more. During the meal each asked where the other was from, and it turned out that the couple were Chinese! He had thought they were on his side, not theirs. Karma again. They continued their meal together with new understanding. This experience totally changed his perspective.

He wanted to continue healing so he then started trying to get to know Chinese people. He tried Chinese food and liked it. When our conference organizer invited Kuno to be with us, he also wanted to set up some lectures for Kuno in the area and offered to let him stay at his house. Kuno told him that he would like to do the lectures, but he wanted to stay with a Chinese family if possible. The organizer said that would be very easy to organize since his foreign-exchange student host family lived nearby, and they just happen to be Chinese! (Coincidence? I think not.) Kuno stayed with the Chinese family before and after the conference and had a wonderful time in their home.

After a couple of days with them, he came to our conference and received your lighter.

At this point in his lecture, he held up your lighter, lit it, and played the little song. He told the story of getting the lighter at the conference, of all the groups he could have been with, of all the wrapped gifts he could have picked, he picked you and yours.

It was a gift, supporting his new path to healing. At the time you picked the gift, you didn't know about his new found attempts at healing this pain in his heart, but you helped the process and supported his new path.

I bet the Dalai Lama had a big belly laugh when Kuno told the full story to him.

It's a full circle thing.

If I were you, I'd be honored to be part of that healing circle.

Alison Sheafor's beautiful handblown glass work, along with that of her talented family, can be seen at their website:

http://members.aol.com/AlboGrnt/webpage/albo.html

"I know worrying works, because none of the stuff
I worried about ever happened."
~ Will Rogers

Chapter 10

MONKEY BUSINESS

After a concert one night, a woman approached me with this story. She promises it's true.

A friend of hers owned a pet monkey. Her friend really loved his monkey in the way that anybody who's ever been attached to a pet will understand. The monkey went almost everywhere with him and was great company.

One day her friend got an offer for an unbelievable opportunity in Europe. One he absolutely couldn't pass up. But what to do about his monkey? He would likely be gone for years and there was no way he could take his pet with him.

He decided to try to find a good home for it, preferably with someone else who already had a monkey. That way he could see if the person really cared about monkeys, and his own pet would have another monkey for company.

But just like people, sometimes monkeys don't like each other. Especially if they're of different species. In addition, finding people who live with and love monkeys is not easy.

So he put an ad in the paper. He put the word out to everybody he could. He put flyers all over town and waited, but nothing happened. He got no response for weeks. Finally, just a week before he was to leave for Europe, he heard of a man who might be interested. The man had a monkey of his own, and was interested in having another one if the monkeys could get along.

The two men met, liked each other, and decided to see if their monkeys were compatible. They put the two monkeys in their cages, at opposite sides of the same room, and watched what happened.

Immediately the monkeys became very agitated. They shrieked and yelled and jumped around their cages. This went on for hours nonstop. The men couldn't really tell what was happening for sure, but it didn't look good. Eventually the monkeys calmed down and were relatively peaceful through the night.

The next day they put the cages a little closer together, and the shrieking began all over again. If anything, it was even worse this time. Both monkeys became extremely agitated, and it was impossible to tell what was going on. Again it lasted all day long.

But the day was coming when the first man had to leave, so there was nothing else to do but keep trying. So the next day they put the cages almost next to each other, and the monkeys went crazy. Absolute chaos. Jumping, screaming, yelling at the top of their lungs for hours. It was bewildering and hard to watch.

The next day the two men decided there was no choice but to find out if these monkeys were going to be able to live together. With great anxiety and trepidation, they opened the cages to see what would happen.

What happened was totally unexpected.

The monkeys leaped out of their cages and instantly, immediately, without the slightest hesitation, hugged each other.

And they didn't let go for three days.

* * *

I was told this story because during my performance I had been emphasizing the importance of touch. As primates, I believe we're hard-wired for a lot of physical contact. As Americans, we don't get much of it. Researchers tell us that other primates (chimps, gorillas, orangutans) spend a couple of hours a day grooming each other: smoothing hair, removing insects from fur, and other hygenic pampering. Additionally, other researchers say that people in Latin and African cultures touch each other an average of 120 times per day. Here in the U.S. of Stress, the number is closer to seven.

My advice is to go home tonight and spend a couple of hours grooming somebody you love. You might experience a lot less shrieking and agitation. Maybe you'll even get a three-day improvement in your relationship.

The woman who shared this story with me, Sharon Kennick, and her partner take women on wilderness, backpacking, and camping adventures near the Grand Canyon. Their website is www.outdooradventureforwomen.com

"A little nonsense now and then is cherished by the wisest men." ~ Roald Dahl

Chapter 11

THE FULL MONTY AT THE AIRPORT

Recently at the Seattle airport I won the Super Special Secret Security lottery. Actually, it's like the opposite of winning the lottery. That little SSSS gets printed on your boarding pass, and you don't even get the fun of scratching off the gray covering. And if you think the regular security line can get long, you should try the SSSS one. Not a good place to have Type A-ness.

So I was crammed into this tight, snaking line with all the other winners, moving at the speed of your average glacier, and the general mood was about what you'd expect for a combination root canal and prostate exam. I felt my own impatience starting to make itself known, and decided I needed a distraction. Just then Clyde (my inner guide) woke up and impishly suggested playing Let's Make A Deal.

So when I finally got to the metal detector, I said in a loud voice to the TSA guy on the other side, "All right, Monty, I'll take Door Number One! What d'ya got for me?"

The guy looked a little startled, tried not to smile, and said very seriously, "Boarding pass, please."

I passed my pass to him and when he motioned me to walk through, I said, "Congratulations, Greg, you've won some lovely gamma radiation—over your entire body!"

Then he said, "Are these your bags sir?"

And I said, "Yes, Monty, do I get to keep them, or do I have to trade them for Door number 2?"

He said, "Sir, we'll have to inspect them, and you'll have to go with this man here to be wanded."

I said, "Wow, Monty, a free inspection AND a wanding! This is incredible. I'm so glad I chose Door Number One."

So then the new Monty says, "Just sit right over here sir and raise your left foot."

I said, "Monty, this is great. Do I get some reflexology with this?"

And he says, "Nope. I'm afraid that was Door Number 2." (This Monty was a slight improvement.)

I said "Darn it, Monty. Well, I guess you can't win everything."

He said "Raise your other foot now sir."

I said, "It's Greg, Monty. You can call me Greg. Especially since this is so personal."

He said, "Okay, stand up, Greg, I have to wand your body now."

I said, "Wow, a full body wand! Monty, this is exceptional. But I can't see you back there. So be careful where you put that thing."

He said, "I'll have to pat you down, now."

I said, "Great, a massage! Monty, what do I have to trade you for this?"

"Nothing sir, it's all part of the service."

I said, "Monty, if you're gonna touch me all over, you really have to call me Greg."

He said, "Please undo your belt buckle now, sir."

I said, "Monty, no man has ever said that to me before. Can't you get the lovely Carol Merrill to do this?"

"Okay sir, you're clean. Your bags are coming."

I said, "Monty, it was all over so quickly."

Just then another TSA guy brought my carry-ons over. And I said, "Wow, I even get to keep my bags! Door number one is fabulous. Hey, did you see anything in there you want to trade for?"

He said, "Those look like some nice headphones."

I said, "Hey, you want 'em? I'll trade 'em for that cool TSA shirt you got on. What do ya say, Monty?"

This Monty just smiled (a little) and said, "Have a good flight, sir."

I said "Hey Monty, what does that TSA stand for anyway?"

He said, "Transportation Security Administration."

I said, "Oh, good. I was starting to think it meant Terribly Serious Ashcroft-impersonator."

"If only I had a little humility, I'd be perfect."
~ *Ted Turner*

Chapter 12

CHOP SUEY, Y'ALL

One evening way back in college my roommate and I wandered over to the dining hall for dinner. In all of New Orleans, a city full of great food and world renowned chefs, Tulane University managed to have the worst place to eat. It was called Bruff Commons, but was more appropriately referred to by us students as Barf Commons.

The specialty of the house was gravy. I guess that way they figured you couldn't tell for sure what you were eating. Or see it, for that matter. Every day it was sitting like a soggy mass of protoplasm on top of whatever else they were serving. Maybe it was a southern thing I just couldn't get used to, but I still don't think my digestive system has ever completely recovered.

My roommate was an architecture student. We had just sat down at the end of a long table with our gravy and whatever else was under it, when a group of eight or ten of his architecture buddies came in for dinner. They were laughing and joking with each other, and since they knew my roommate, they sat down to eat with us.

I was at the end of the table, and I found myself sitting across from an oriental student. The two of us were the only ones not joining in the verbal give and take, and in my case it was because I didn't know any of these guys. I glanced at this boy across from me, trying to gauge if he was shy. Or maybe, I thought, he just doesn't know English very well. We had a lot of Asian students on campus, and the few I had spoken with seemed self-conscious about their English. I wondered what country he was from. China? Korea? Vietnam?

He and I ate in silence for several minutes, and my empathy for him grew. It seemed a shame that he couldn't — or wouldn't — join the conversation with his classmates. I knew how it felt to be different and left out, and imagined that's what he was feeling. Finally I decided to break the ice. With the sole intention of making him feel more comfortable, I casually asked, "So where ya from, anyway?"

He looked up at me and with the biggest, fattest southern accent you ever heard, said, "Mississippi. You want to pass the buttah?"

I almost choked on my gravy.

* * *

A few years later I found myself in the Big Apple as a tourist. I'd been to the top of the Empire State Building as a teenager, and I wanted to see it again, so I headed up there. After taking in the view for awhile, I made my way back to the elevator. There was only one other person waiting to go down. She was an elderly woman, and as she thanked the guard I could tell she had a strong German accent. We boarded the elevator, and since it was a long ride down and I like to meet foreigners, I asked her if she was from Germany.

"Ya, " she said, and smiled.

I asked her what she did there, and she proudly replied in her thick accent, "I've owned a restaurant for 30 years."

"Really!" I said. "I've been to Germany and I love the food there." At which point I proceeded to rattle off all the dishes I'd eaten, including bratwurst, wiener schnitzel, and God knows what else. When I finally finished my list, hoping I'd impressed her just a little, I asked, "So do you serve any of those in your restaurant?"

"No, " she smiled. "It's a Chinese restaurant."

Old joke:

Have you heard about that new German-Chinese restaurant?

The food's great, but an hour later you're hungry for power.

"There are moments when art almost attains the dignity
of manual labor." ~ Oscar Wilde

Chapter 13

ROCK STAR WAXES POETIC

I love it when my narrow-minded illusions get shattered with a big, fat surprise. Today I really got it how easily I form silly assumptions about people.

I was in Norwalk, Connecticut, and was browsing through a local weekly paper over lunch at a local restaurant. I had it in my head that I would catch a train into NYC to catch a Broadway play of some sort. But my eye caught a blurb announcing that Patti Smith, the rock-and-roller, was giving a free poetry reading at the Westport library. The date was today, the time was an hour from now, and the library just happened to be a mile down the street. I thought, why not check this out. I can always leave.

The only thing I knew about Patti Smith was that she was, or at least had been, classified as a "punk rocker," a genre I never had warmed up to very much. I'd heard maybe a few seconds of her music here and there on the radio back in the '70s or '80s. I also thought she was maybe married to John McEnroe, the tennis player, but then again, maybe not. I wasn't sure. (Nope—that was Patty Smythe.) I definitely had never heard anything about her writing poetry.

It was a beautiful day in Westport, so I finished my lunch and moseyed on over to the library. Sure enough, a moderate sized meeting room was filling up. I grabbed a seat and waited as all 250 or so seats were taken, and then as people stood along the walls and out into the hall. Finally, right on time, she was introduced and out she came.

She looked a lot like what I thought I remembered. Long wildish hair, jeans (or maybe dark pants), a tight cap covering most of her head, no makeup, very slender, and serious. But then, as if to shake me up on purpose, she smiled a big, brilliant smile that lit up the room. She began to speak in a clear, intelligent voice with a most beguiling, charming, and self-effacing sense of humor.

For the next hour she continued to charm, educate, entertain, and amuse us, and especially me. She read poetry, played a couple of songs on guitar, and ad-libbed a refreshing, disarming stream-of-consciousness patter. She read poems about her best friend Robert Mapplethorpe, the controversial photographer who died of AIDS. She read poems about Picasso and Georgia O'Keefe, artists whose lives inspired her. She talked about growing up in a rural town where books and the library were her salvation. She read poems about Joan of Arc and Jesus. She told us how she was fascinated by their humanity, and inspired by their sacrifice. I was impressed. She is a genuine word artist.

Her poetry required some concentration on my part — her poems are complex and challenging, and sometimes hard to follow. They remind me a little of Salvador Dali paintings: easier with an interpreter. But there is no denying the force and the beauty of her word constructions.

What struck me the most, however, was her obvious connection to life, and to the sacredness of it. I wasn't prepared for this at all, and it lifted me up to a place of quiet joy. In prefacing one poem, she spoke of her reaction to the Heaven's Gate suicides a few years ago, and how she was so upset by them, because all we really have here on this planet is our life, our work, our love, and each other. And it's such a shame to waste it. (My words, hers were more eloquent.) It was like I'd been to church and heard a powerful sermon.

This was an hour of thoughtful conversation from a master of communication. She inspired me to think, to question, and especially to feel. And needless to say, to totally reexamine my opinions about "punk rock," or any artist or genre I'm not familiar with. (I'm sure Patti Smith hates being classified. I know I do.)

On top of all that, it was just a mile down the road, and I didn't even have to take the train to Manhattan or buy an expensive Broadway ticket. I did however, buy a book of her poetry. You can't get it all on just one listen.

To be yourself in a world that is constantly trying to make
you something else is the greatest accomplishment.
~ Ralph Waldo Emerson

Chapter 14

STAND LIKE MOUNTAIN,
MOVE LIKE WATER

A few years ago I was invited to open a wellness conference with a concert, and I decided to stick around for a couple of days to see if I could learn anything. The next day I went to a presentation by a speaker and wellness expert named Brian Luke Seaward. His talk was fantastic, and I happened to have a couple of songs that related directly to it. Afterward I stuck my hand in the crowd of people around him, introduced myself, and asked if I could send him some songs. He said sure.

I sent them off, and after about three weeks I got a letter back in the mail. Luke wrote that he enjoyed my songs and offered an idea for another one. His new book was coming out soon, and he'd always thought the title of his book — taken from an old tai chi saying — would make a great song: *Stand Like Mountain, Move Like Water.*

I loved the title, so I called him and told him I'd like to take a crack at writing it. He said great, and since I was going to be in Denver near where he lives, we decided to meet and talk it over. We got together and fortunately hit it off right away. Luke is a great guy, and for a charismatic speaker, quite easy to be with and talk to. We tossed around a few vague ideas for the song, and I went home to write it. For the next ten months or so, I basically got nowhere.

Then one day I was sitting in my living room in Kansas City reading the paper. By chance I stumbled on an in-depth article — an entire half page — about a woman named Nien Cheng and her book, *Life and Death in Shanghai.* The article recounted how during Mao's Cultural Revolution in the '60s, Nien Cheng had been thrown into prison, essentially for being an educated woman. There were some other factors like her religion (Christian) and having worked for a western company (Shell Oil) that also played a part.

In the middle of the night she had been dragged out of her home by Mao's Red Guards, who smashed all of her possessions, took her teenage daughter away, then dragged her off to prison. She was thrown into a tiny cell with no trial, no idea what she had done, no idea how long she might be there, and no contact with the outside world.

For the next 6 and a half years she endured unbelievable deprivation, humiliation, degradation, and interrogation. Mao's Guards thought that by putting her in prison, they could get her to confess to crimes she did not commit. They thought they would be able to control her.

But Nien Cheng turned out to be too strong.

Her captors could definitely control her physically, but what they discovered was they could not control her mind, her emotions, or her spirit. By turning their own rhetoric and distorted logic back on them, she resisted all attempts to get her to sign false confessions, and she endured everything they did to her.

After six and a half years, the political climate changed, and Nien Cheng was finally able to get out of prison. At this point she was 63 years old. Being a small Asian woman to begin with, and having experienced nearly seven years of very little food, physically she was not in the best of shape. But emotionally and mentally she was still strong.

I don't know about you, but whenever I read about someone like Nien Cheng, I wonder what they have inside that makes them able to survive this kind of insanity. I wonder if there's anything I can learn from them. I was greatly inspired by Nien Cheng's determination, courage, and grace. She was so strong, she could adapt to what they did to her. Her tremendous inner strength gave her outer flexibility.

Inner strength, outer flexibility.

Stand Like Mountain, Move Like Water!

There it was. So I hurried over to Nashville and met with my writing partner, Richard Helm. Up to this point Richard and I had written a number of songs, but they were all funny songs, nothing serious. I brought this idea to him anyway, he was jazzed about it, and the song really came pretty quickly. We were both happy with how it turned out, so I hustled back to K.C. and sent a copy off to Luke Seaward, who (as you might remember) had given me the title.

A couple of days later, Luke called me. I could hear the excitement in his voice. He told me he really liked what we had done with the song, but he had a question. By any chance, was this song about Nien Cheng, from China?

I replied that it was, and asked how on earth he knew that?

"Oh," he said. "She's a friend of mine."

Postscript

When Nien Cheng was released from prison, she found out that her daughter had been pressured so intensely to give evidence against her that she committed suicide by jumping off a building. That was the story, anyway. There's some evidence that she may have been pushed.

Nien eventually was able to get out of China and emigrate to the States. She settled in Washington DC, where Luke lived and taught at the time. Somehow they connected and became friends.

Through Luke's introduction, I was able to meet Nien Cheng on a couple of separate trips to Washington. She fed me tea and cookies in her apartment, and even though she was in her late 80s, she was vital and full of energy. She read several newspapers each day and still managed all her own affairs. She still drove her little Honda all over Washington. I could barely keep up with her.

On my next trip there she took me to lunch at her favorite Chinese restaurant. (Although she has no love for the government of her native country, she still loves her native food.) Over a long lunch she told me many stories about growing up in China and about being in prison. She even told me a few things she was not able to put in the book, for fear of reprisals.

After a couple of hours of being mesmerized by her stories, and as always, inspired by her grace and dignity, I asked her if she had a philosophy of life.

"Oh yes," she said. "I have a philosophy of life."

"Would you share it with me?" I asked.

"Of course," she replied. "Always be in control of your own life. And always be optimistic."

"That's beautiful, Nien," I said. "But you were in prison. What do you mean by always be in control of your own life?"

"Always have a plan," she replied. "Even when I was in prison,

I had a plan."

"Really. What was your plan?" I asked.

"My plan was to live longer than Mao."

Nien Cheng's book "Life and Death in Shanghai" is still in print and is simply gripping. An excellent book.

Brian Luke Seaward has many outstanding books in print, including "Stand Like Mountain, Flow Like Water." He can be reached at his website: www.brianlukeseaward.net

STAND LIKE MOUNTAIN, MOVE LIKE WATER
(Greg Tamblyn, Richard Helm, Brian Luke Seaward)

At the foot of a mountain, in a bamboo cafe
Sat an old Asian lady with eyes full of grace
I felt myself drawn to her calm, quiet way
And as her story started to flow
I was carried away

She told of a night when soldiers appeared
And chained her in darkness for seven long years
There's a wall in her country a thousand miles long
And they wrapped it around her
For thinking and speaking all wrong

Stand like mountain, move like water
Earth and heaven have this to offer
Strength will flow from life with honor
Stand like mountain, move like water

She knew in her heart she'd committed no crime
And a story to tell is what kept her alive
In a cell with no windows she nurtured the seed
That one day the light would shine in
And people would see

I thought how her life was so different from mine
And the insight that came has remained in my mind
Here is a woman who knows who she is
Through good times and bad she's the same
The way that she lives

Stand like mountain, move like water
Earth and heaven have this to offer
Strength will flow from life with honor
Stand like mountain, move like water

At the foot of a mountain in a bamboo cafe
We bowed to each other and I made my way
And I carry with me like the seeds on the wind
Her spirit and her story to tell, and so it begins

Stand like mountain, move like water
Stand like mountain, move like water

"Mix a little foolishness with your serious plans:
it's lovely to be silly at the right moment. "
~ Horace

Chapter 15

OU'EST LE SALLE DE BAIN?
(Where Is The Bathroom?)

My sister and her husband joined the Peace Corps the year after they got married. They were sent to the Ivory Coast, a former French colony. When their two year African hitch was up they had become fluent in French, they had the little bit of money the Peace Corps gave them, so they thought, *Hey — let's go live in Paris!*

But all they could afford in Paris was a tiny, two-room apartment. And the operative word here is "tiny." One room was a bedroom, with a double bed in it, and just about enough room to walk around it. That was the whole bedroom.

The other room was the kitchen. A little, efficiency-type kitchen. And that was it, the whole apartment.

So, you might be thinking, *Where was the bathroom?*

The bathroom was not down the hall. Nor was it shared with another apartment.

The bathroom was in the kitchen.

In the corner of the kitchen was a little alcove with a rickety little door in front of it. Inside the alcove was a commode, and above the commode was a shower head. That was it — the whole bathroom. But it was so small that when you sat on the commode your knees kept the rickety little door from closing.

Also in the kitchen was a small, square table. And if four people, who weren't very big, arranged themselves just exactly right, they could squeeze in around it and have a meal together. This happened often because nobody had any money. So you might be thinking, *What if somebody had to go to the bathroom during dinner? As does happen.*

Now here's what I consider a great example of creative problem solving.

If someone had to go during dinner, the person would move to the alcove, and assume the position behind the door. Then the rest of the people at the table, which was maybe an arm's length away, would pound on the table, and sing at the top of their lungs to give the person some privacy. This went on for as long as it took, until they got the "all clear." (Flush, gurgle.)

Needless to say, this made for some funny dinners. And because the alcove was about the size of a phone booth (or smaller) the code for this became, "I gotta make a phone call!"

Of course the next question was, "Well, is it local or long distance?" (In other words, how long are we gonna be singing?)

Now that's really thinking outside the john.

"If you find yourself in a hole, the first thing to do is stop diggin' ". ~ Will Rogers

Chapter 16

THE SEWERS OF PARIS

My French friends looked at me like I was from Mars when I told them I wanted to tour the sewers of Paris. You'd have thought I'd wanted to eat escargot with Velveeta, or hang glide off the Eiffel Tower. The sewer tour was not something they had ever thought of doing, although they'd heard that you could. Like most natives of a place, there were a great many things in their own city they had never seen or done. Probably because these things would always be available and so there was no hurry. That, and the fact that there is a lot to see and do in Paris. And maybe some of it might be more interesting than the sewers.

Museums, for example. I'm sure no one person has ever seen all the museums of Paris — there are just too many. The French are justifiably proud of their history — Paris has been a city for about 2000 years or so — and so they tend to hang on to their old stuff. If it survives a few wars and nothing else comes up, they usually make a museum out of it.

Especially if the stuff ever had anything whatsoever to do with anyone who might have slept with or known or even got a glimpse of Napoleon. Napoleon is to the French what aliens are to Steven Spielberg. His tomb alone is a testament to the endless fascination and wonderment they feel for him. It's big, it's gaudy, and of course, it's in a museum. I'm not all that up on my French history, but I think he might have been the last French General who actually won anything. So in spite of the fact that he was kind of a nut, they like him.

Anyway, my friends good-naturedly humored me and agreed to accompany me into the Parisian sewers. I had read in the guidebook that it was actually quite interesting. There's a guide who takes you through and shows you the construction growth, history and architecture of Paris from underneath. This knowledge would, needless to say, make you enormously popular at parties. (It also brings up one of the great job titles of all time: Sewer Guide. I'd love to get my hands on one of those badges.)

So the four of us arranged to meet at the entrance to the sewer tour the next morning at the appointed hour. Three of us arrived on time, and as we waited for our late friend, we began to look around. There was a ticket kiosk by a gate which opened onto some steps leading downward and, presumably, to the sewers. To our supreme disappointment (well, mine anyway), the kiosk was quite obviously closed, the gate was just as obviously locked, and there was a big sign in French that said the sewers were not open for touring during this early part of January. Needless to say, we were all bummed. (Well, me anyway.)

So we stood there by the kiosk waiting for our tardy friend and began to make alternate plans. We were so engrossed in our discussion we didn't notice that an odd thing was happening. Just as our friend arrived we looked up in amazement to see that 25 or 30 people had lined up behind us, patiently waiting and expecting to get into the sewers! Since we were standing by the ticket booth, they evidently thought we knew something they didn't, even though everything was locked up tight as a drum and the sign plainly said no go.

This struck me as pretty funny, and before my friends could set our fellow sewer-seekers straight, I suggested we just move away a few feet and watch what happened.

What happened was that the laws of inertia and denial came into effect. These people did not want to move. They were confused by our departure. They had lost their leaders. They did not want to believe the obvious or admit they had made a kind of silly assumption. So they stood there for at least fifteen more minutes, not wanting reality to set in. Finally, in grudging acceptance and obvious disappointment, they began drifting away.

I felt a little like the man behind the curtain in The Wizard of Oz. It would have made a good Candid Camera.

What this all goes to prove is that if you even just *look* like you know what you're doing, people will follow you anywhere. Even down the drain.

*"I love to think of nature as an unlimited broadcasting
system through which God speaks to us every hour,
if we will only tune in." ~ George Washington Carver.*

Chapter 17

MY INNER WIMP MEETS THE
INCA TRAIL

I got in touch with my inner wimp recently, hiking the Inca Trail in Peru. I discovered he's a lucky and ignorant inner wimp, too.

It's true that the Inca Trail is a challenging hike, and yes I did finish it with all my body parts intact. But some things definitely got put into perspective.

In case you're geographically challenged, the Inca Trail is in the Andes Mountains. They run like a spine up the length of South America, and are some of the steepest, most rugged mountains on the planet. Several hundred years ago the Incas built an amazing network of trails through a large chunk of them. These Incas, being practical people and in incredibly good shape, did not waste time with any silly, labor-saving devices like, say, switchbacks. Nope, it was straight up, and straight down, Bub. As a result, in many places the Inca Trail is hundreds of meters of actual stone stair steps going steeply up, and then straight down the other side. In addition, much of it rises between 11,000 and 14,000 feet. Which means there's not a lot of oxygen to suck in. Or at least a lot less than a sea level guy like me is used to.

So there I am, slowly working my way up and down these endless, ancient stone stair-masters, wearing my expensive hiking boots, carrying all of about eight or ten pounds in my daypack. I'm drinking lots of coca tea, and I'm feeling pretty good about the fact that I'm actually doing the hike, not getting sick from altitude or giving up or anything.

But then our guides come along — Marco, Juan, and Willy — gliding past me with encouraging words, like I'm a kid learning to ride a two-wheeler.

They cruise up and down these stone stairways at will, as far as I can tell never even needing a breather. And I'm thinking, *Wow — these guys are really in great shape.*

But here's the kicker. We're camping and hiking with porters. This means neither we nor our guides are carrying anything heavy. For our nine hikers plus three guides, we have 16 porters and one cook. The porters carry basically everything heavier than an energy bar and some water: the tents, the tables, the chairs, the food, the latrine, and even all of our extra clothes. So each of these porters straps on a bundle of stuff that looks like the Beverly Hillbillies' truck on moving day. And to assemble and carry these huge bundles, all they use are ropes and cloth straps. No fancy high-tech backpacks. They don't wear hiking boots either. These guys are poor, off season farmers. They've never owned a pair of hiking boots. They wear sandals. Sandals!

And you know what else? These are not big guys. They're thin and wiry. They could maybe make your junior high school football team. But they hustle up and down these mountain trails like they have bionic legs or something. Frequently even running. With 80 pounds of hand tied camp gear tied on their backs. In sandals.

So that, amigos, is why I feel like a wimp.

The reason I feel like a lucky, ignorant wimp is that these porters earn maybe $40 or $50 for 4 days of this portering. That's total, not per day. And they're happy to get it. They're also some of the sweetest, humblest, most generous people I've ever met. They were even gracious about lugging my little travel guitar along, and treating it like a baby. They pitched camp and broke camp every day, frequently in the mud and rain. They woke us up every morning with hot tea delivered to our tents.

On the morning of my birthday, they surprised me in our breakfast tent with a big chocolate covered birthday cake, which one of them had carried for three days. (It was chewy, but good.) After a spirited rendition of Happy Birthday by our group, the porters sang approximately 25 verses of some Peruvian birthday song in Spanish about kissing a skeleton in a cemetery. The whole time they were grinning like crazy and clapping in rhythm as they stood and sang in the morning drizzle around the entrance to the tent. It was fantastic, warm, funny and we all loved it.

These porters carried our gear and pampered us for four days, so that we could huff and puff up and down the famous Inca Trail, and gaze and gawk at some of the most spectacular scenery in the world: high snowy peaks; deep gorges and ravines with waterfalls; beautiful, mysterious stone ruins of Inca cities and religious sites. So that we could descend through quiet, beautiful cloud forest and suddenly, from the top of the mountain behind us, hear a spell-binding solo flute played by our guide, Marco.

So that we could be resting comfortably during a break and be amused by the sight of a young girl trying to drive a flock of noisy, unruly turkeys past us down the trail. So that we could break into uncontrollable laughter as our assistant guide and bird expert, Juan, with his comedic plastic body and rubber face, jumped up and ran at the turkeys yelling, "Silencio!" Which of course sent them running in all directions and squawking even louder.

So that we could stop and marvel at hummingbirds, kestrels, tanagers, and orchids. So that we could sit cozily in our dining tent, lingering over a wonderful dinner with hot spiced wine, singing, joking, and laughing, as Juan took every possible opportunity to stand and announce, "I want to celebrate this moment!"

So that after 4 days of hard hiking we could climb the final few steps of the Trail and emerge through the ancient Sun Gate high on the mountain, looking down on one of the most dramatic sights anywhere: the awesome stone city of Machu Picchu, surrounded by steep granite mountains of indescribable beauty. (I'm sure you've seen the pictures.)

So that we could sit, deeply moved, listening to Marco as he was brought to tears by his passion for this sacred place, for his own Inca heritage, and his pain at the history of Spanish exploitation.

I'm really grateful to those porters. I feel changed by this trek. Or maybe I should say, reawakened. I got back in touch with how rejuvenating it is to be away from all the stuff and the stimuli of modern life. To be pushing my body past its usual limits. To be deep into nature amidst breathtaking beauty. To have fascinating new sights and sounds and things to learn every day. To experience a culture different from our own, and to find it warm and welcoming. To enjoy the daily camaraderie of a group of new, but like-minded friends.

As two members of our group remarked later, time passed so much more slowly than at home, more like when we were kids and the days stretched on forever. I got in touch with how much I need that in my life.

Oh, you can absolutely go to Peru and have a magical experience without hiking the Trail. The ruins, the people, the guides, the scenery, the history, the spirituality, all of these things are worth the trip and can be transforming in themselves. People do it all the time and love it.

But my inner wimp needed the hike.

Postscript

It says a lot about the Incan stonemason talents that many of these trails are still in good shape. In fact, the overwhelming impression I have of the Incas is that they were geniuses with stone. They built structures so well designed and so precise that 500 years later a remarkable amount of their work is still standing, and still able to withstand an 8.5 scale earthquake. I found myself constantly marveling at how perfectly they fit together huge, highly polished blocks of rock with no mortar. The trapezoidal shape of their walls, doors, and windows is so effective at resisting large earth tremors, that scientists, architects, and builders from all over the world (most notably Japan) come here to study their techniques.

That alone would make these ancient stone cities worth marveling at. But somehow they also managed to design them with an aesthetic eye, incorporating vitally significant elements of their spirituality and astronomy into the structures. Frequently you come upon a whole stone city designed in the shape of a puma (Cuzco, for example), a snake, or a condor. These three animals represent the three worlds of Incan spirituality. The lower world is represented by the snake, which also stands for wisdom. The puma symbolizes Pachamama, or mother earth. And the condor represents the heavens, or the journey to the afterlife. All you have to do is keep your eyes open to see them again and again in these stones.

You can also find plenty of astronomical structures. Much like other ancient stone builders, the Incas placed a lot of importance on the solstices and equinoxes. Not only for spiritual reasons, but for their highly developed agriculture. If the Incas were geniuses with stone, they were downright brilliant at growing food. Their intricate system of irrigated mountain terraces, designed for growing different plants in slightly different elevations, enabled them to feed everyone in their empire, with a lot left over. There was essentially no hunger and no poverty.

Of course, you could also get your lips and tongue chopped off for telling a lie, but every culture has its little inconveniences.

"If you don't believe God has a sense of humor, just look at your neighbor." ~ Will Rogers

Chapter 18

THE DANGERS OF NETWORKING

Sometimes you can just try too hard.

I think that's what happened after a I did a particularly good concert in a western city one night. A very lovely woman approached me and handed me her card. She told me her name (let's call her Blanche), and said she did seminars on male-female communication. She thought perhaps we might be able to help each other, or in some way network a bit, maybe even do some work together.

I felt my ears prick up when she said the magic words, "male-female communication." (I have so much to learn.) So I suggested we meet for lunch the next day before I left town. She agreed and told me about a restaurant that sounded good.

The next day I met her at noon, and Blanche was dressed to kill. I definitely got the impression that she wanted to make a good impression, if you get my drift. Sometimes you can just tell — and I didn't even need any courses in body language to know it. So we ordered some food and soon the salads came. We were chatting and munching, and I was enjoying her conversation.

Then the main course showed up. I couldn't recognize what she'd ordered, so I asked her what it was. She said excitedly, "Oh, you have to try this! These are green chile wontons, I get them every time I come here, and they're fabulous!" And with that, she took a bite.

What happened next was surreal. She immediately turned red and started whooping. Not coughing, not choking, but *whooping*. Like, "Whoop! Whoop! Whoop!" She was definitely having some kind of reaction, but what? I couldn't tell, and it scared the dumplings out of me.

I asked her what was wrong, and could I help? Should I call 911? She shook her head and kept whooping. Then she stood up, still whooping, quickly now, every second or so. By now the whoops were really loud, her face was quite red, and everyone in the place was staring at us. They were looking at her with concern and fear. They were looking at me like, *What have you done to her?* And, *Why aren't you helping?*

But I had no clue what to do. Heimlich maneuver? She shook her head. Hamlisch maneuver? (Singing "The Way We Were" until they throw up.) No, no time for humor.

Now she was whooping louder and faster and I was really getting worried.

Then suddenly she ran into the ladies restroom. Now the whooping was echoing off the tile walls in there and reverberating through the restaurant, "Whooooop! Whoooooop! Whoooooop!"

A minute later a couple of concerned waitresses scurried in there to help, and I felt a drop in my anxiety level. Still not knowing what to do I sat down, feeling helpless, worried, and stared at from all corners of the restaurant.

Finally, the volume and frequency of whooping in the restroom began to subside a bit: "whoop.............. whoop.............whoop.......," and eventually stopped altogether. Then there was silence for about 5 or 10 minutes.

Those few minutes felt like an hour. She emerged from the restroom and walked over to the table, looking red, exhausted, and all wrung out. I stood up and asked if she was okay, and she said yes, but she was so embarrassed. I told her there was no need to be embarrassed, but did she need anything? Should I call somebody?

No no, she said, she was fine, but she just felt so foolish. She thought I must think her a real idiot to tell me how great those things were and then they almost killed her.

Gosh no, I said, you just had a reaction. It could have happened to anybody. Don't worry about it. The main thing is you're okay.

But she just wouldn't let it go. She said she just felt so stupid, and sat down. You must think I'm such a *dope*, she said. And as she said the word *dope*, she was moving her arms down for emphasis, and her right hand hit her fork, which was buried in her salad.

It was Murphy's Law in vivid, technicolor 3-D.

Salad sprayed everywhere. It flew all over the table. It was on her dress, in her lap, in her hair. Basically everywhere but on me. And at that point, there was nothing to do but laugh. Well, anyway I laughed. I can't remember if she laughed. I hope so.

But for some reason, I never heard from her again.

"The true joy in life is being used for a purpose recognized by yourself as a mighty one. It is being a force of nature instead of a selfish feverish little cloud of ailments and grievances complaining that the world will not devote itself to making you happy. I want to be thoroughly used up when I die; the harder I work the more I live. Life is no brief candle to me. It is a sort of burning torch which I want to make burn as brightly as possible before handing it on to future generations." ~ George Bernard Shaw, Man and Superman

Chapter 19

OUT FRONT IN THE OUTBACK

On the highway to Alice Springs in the Australian outback, an aboriginal woman wearing only a skirt tried to throw herself under our bus. We could see her from a distance lying on the highway waiting to get run over. Fortunately our driver was able to slow down and avoid her. But just as we approached she jumped up and tried to run under the bus. There was a man attempting to prevent her from doing this, but she was pretty determined, and we just barely missed her.

We were a little shaken up, so our driver gave us a short talk on alcoholism among the aboriginals. Evidently they have little tolerance for alcohol, and evidently in many towns there is little or no employment opportunity for them. In some places I guess it's pretty grim. I'd heard Alice was one of those places.

Before this, all the Aboriginals we'd met had been our teachers and guides. We'd just spent several days at one of their sacred sites called Uluru, an enormous monolithic piece of red granite in the heart of the continent, rising seemingly out of nowhere from the flat desert. It's so big, so red, and so unlike anything else that you can't stop staring at it. It takes at least half a day to walk around it. People die all the time trying to climb it.

The Aboriginal guides there had taught us about their myths and culture. We learned about hunting, gathering, food making and some of their sacred history. We learned how to throw spears and paint with dots. We got a sense of how they have managed to thrive for 60,000 years in one of the hottest, bleakest, most barren and inhospitable places on the planet. I developed a respect bordering on awe for their survival skills. I also became quite enamored with and connected to the land itself, which I wasn't expecting. Everyone in our group felt this way.

That's why it was so doubly strange to see this woman on the highway. We hadn't encountered any Aboriginals like her. But later, in Alice, we did in fact see many more who were on the down-and-outs.We started to get a glimpse of the struggle they face coming to terms with a white culture and lifestyle so different from their own ancient one.

The next day we took a day trip from Alice Springs to Santa Teresa, a small, rural aboriginal community. On the way out of town we encountered a "road train," which is the local name for three semi trailers hitched together behind a truck cab. We were on a two lane highway, which is all they have in the outback, so it passed quite close to us. It does look like a small train, and as it flew by us in the opposite direction the wind blast felt like a small explosion. In the vast Northern Territory desert there are almost no speed limits and no restrictions on how many hours a driver can be at the wheel. In consideration of all these factors, I decided to put on my seat belt.

We turned off the highway on to a dirt road. The good news was no more danger from speeding, hulking road trains. The bad news was we had 80 km of a very bumpy dirt track to cover. The good news was we had a fascinating video of kangaroos to watch on the bus. The bad news was one of the kangaroo joeys (pups) got eaten by a dingo. Nature is so cruel.

Just when I thought things couldn't get any more interesting, something else happened. Arriving in Santa Teresa, we met an impressive aboriginal woman named Agnes who runs a spiritual center. It's in the same building where she attended school as a little girl, learning English and other subjects from the nuns. She showed us a few of her paintings, speaking beautifully, interpreting their spiritual meanings for us.

Santa Teresa is a humble place, reminding me more than anything of some American Indian reservations. The streets are dirt, and the homes are small and simple. After seeing many inebriated aboriginals in Alice Springs, I confess I wasn't prepared for a woman with the depth and dignity of Agnes here in tiny Santa Teresa. I was further caught off guard when Agnes told us some of her life journey and her own struggle with alcoholism.

With her quietly commanding presence she related how, while living in Alice, all the pressures of life built to a point that she hit bottom and started drinking. She told us there was a voice in her head urging her to throw herself under a truck or a bus and kill herself. The voice said she would be happier if she did that. Her husband was alcoholic too, and she felt hopeless in those days. The voice in her head was persuasive and lasted a long time.

But somehow she resisted it, and one day her sister suggested she write down all her negative thoughts and sins on a piece of paper and put it in the God bottle. So she did. For a long time she was afraid someone would read the piece of paper and discover her shame.

Some time later she was standing by the stove, and felt a sweet breeze on her cheek. She heard a new voice telling her to burn the paper in the God bottle. As soon as this was done she felt an immediate cleansing. Her grief and hopelessness were washed away, replaced by an overpowering sense of love. The voice in her head telling her to kill herself was gone. She decided to join Alcoholics Anonymous.

Occasionally there was still some pain in her body. She thought this must be the pain of Jesus, and that she needed to help others as he had. So she came back to her village and started her center, where she gives assistance to families grappling with alcoholism. She also helps people individually, using the aboriginal practice of "smoking." This is like smudging in native North America. She burns a local grass to make the smoke and pass it over the body. As she does this, she feels the person's hands to sense where the spirit is out of kilter, and tries to correct that for them.

Even more impressively, if that's possible, she has been instrumental in one of the most beautiful art projects I have ever seen. Inside the small Catholic church in Santa Teresa are stunning large murals depicting a convergence of both aboriginal and Christian stories. These include the creation stories, and several of the Jesus stories told with aboriginal characters in local settings. It's hard to overstate the beauty of these paintings. They're simply spellbinding.

Agnes explained some of these aboriginal stories for us: how the world was created, how the crow and the mynah got their distinctive colors and voices, and how the lizards got their markings. These stories are vividly depicted on the walls, along with many others, like the birth and baptism of Jesus in aboriginal settings. The synthesis of these stories from two cultures and the unexpected beauty of the artwork led me to a profound sense of reverence and hope. Hope for these people, so forgotten for so long, and hope for the next generation of their children. At least the ones in Santa Teresa.

All by themselves, Agnes and this church art were worth our entire trip to the Outback.

PART TWO

Inner Travel

"The whole problem can be stated quite simply by asking,
'Is there a meaning to music?' My answer would be, 'Yes.'
And 'Can you state in so many words what the meaning
is?' My answer to that would be, 'No.'"
~ Aaron Copland

Chapter 20

SAVING THE WORLD FROM WHINY VICTIM LOVE SONGS

In the very funny movie, "High Fidelity," the character played by John Cusack looks into the camera and asks, with obvious humorous angst, *"What came first, the music or the misery? People worry about kids watching violent TV shows and movies, playing with violent video games. They worry that some sort of culture of violence will take them over. But nobody worries about kids listening to thousands, literally thousands, of songs about heartbreak, rejection, pain, misery, and loss. Did I listen to pop music because I was miserable? Or was I miserable because I listened to pop music?"*

When I moved to Nashville to become a songwriter in the '80s, I found I had to start paying close attention to lyrics. In the country music market, the story's always been the thing. When I was pitching songs to publishers, every word got scrutinized.

So as I started paying more attention to the lyrics of songs, I noticed something interesting. There were quite a lot of truly wonderful love songs out there. But there were all these other songs, basically masquerading as love songs, that were really about taking hostages. About some kind of emotional bondage or slavery. Seriously dysfunctional songs.

A point of clarification here. Sad songs are really okay. You lose somebody, you feel lousy. It hurts. You need to grieve. Sad songs can help us do that. But when you cross the line and start *asking* for pain, then you've decended into the Realm of Real Sickness. Here's the thing: as John Cusack's character says, there are literally *thousands* of songs out there that do just that! They float around the airwaves, malls, and movie theaters, infecting our consciousness, depressing our immune systems. They burn their whiny lyrics into our brains when our guard is down because we're grooving on the melody, dancing to the rhythms, or we're just too dumb to know better.

So, my friends, as a public service, I've been collecting them. For the edification and enlightenment of not only my own personal self, but of you too, if you're ready. I say, "Enough! It's time to stand up and take back our music. Let us refuse to be any further infected and afflicted by these insidious agents of victimhood! It's time we consign these songs to their rightful place in the world of entertainment: material for comedy!"

So to that end, I offer some of my favorite song titles and lyric lines for your education and amusement. These are actual, real songs, that somewhere, sometime, somebody actually recorded. (If I could get permission to print all the lyrics, I would. But I'm sure you'll understand that publishers are a teensy bit reluctant to share their lyrics for the purpose of open ridicule.) Even so, I'm sure you'll agree, the titles and phrases alone are wonderful.

Here then, are some of my favorites. I have hundreds more, trust me.

Beauty is in the eye of the beerholder

If you leave me, can I come too?

I married her because she looks like you

It ain't easy bein' easy

**Get your tongue out of my mouth,
I'm kissing you goodbye**

**Treat me like a fool, treat me cruel,
but love me**

**She was pure as the new fallen snow,
but she drifted**

I still love her body,
but I think I've lost her mind

She feels like a new man tonight

If heartaches were wine I'd be
drunk all the time

I'm working on my next broken heart

How can I breathe without you?

I wish that I could hurt that way again

Momma get the hammer, there's a fly
on papa's head

If I'd shot you when I met you, I'd be
out of prison by now

You're the reason our kids are so ugly

He hit me and it felt like a kiss

If you won't leave me
I'll find someone who will

I'm so miserable without you,
it's like you were here

If you gotta hurt somebody, please hurt me

Make me do right, make me do wrong,
I'm your puppet

It's hard to kiss the lips at night that chew
your ass out all day long

Friends, some people have a mission. Some people have a
vision. Some people have a cause. I have a crusade. I'm Saving the
World from Whiny Victim Love Songs.   Thank you for helping.

*"There's a part of every thing that wants to become itself;
the tadpole into the frog, the chrysalis into the butterfly,
a damaged human being into a whole one.
That is spirituality. "* ~ Ellen Bass

Chapter 21

SIX MONTHS TO LIVE:
THE STORY OF EVY MCDONALD

During 1990 I lived in the Cayman Islands, working as an entertainer at a posh resort. Despite the exotic, laid back lifestyle, it was a period of great uncertainty in my life, and after a few months I started experiencing loneliness and a severe depression. One night I listened to an audio book by Bernie Siegel called Peace, Love, and Healing. In it, Bernie recounted the story of a woman named Evy McDonald, and it changed my life.

In 1980, Evy was diagnosed with A.L.S., "Lou Gehrig's Disease." By the time the doctors had figured out what the problem was, the disease was quite advanced. In Evy's words, she was "a bowl of jello in a wheelchair." The doctor came into her hospital room and gave her the news that the best she could hope for would be about six months. Evy had a master's degree in nursing and knew this was a fatal illness.

She went home and became enraged about her situation for a couple of days. Then Evy had a thought: even though she was dying, even though her body just barely worked anymore, and even though she only had six months left to live, was there something she could do to make the most out of her last six months?

So she came up with a plan. Evy sat in front of a mirror naked and looked at herself. She'd had polio as a child, so she had two withered limbs. In addition, she'd been overweight her whole life. And now, she was dying of a wasting disease. Evy sat there and experienced all the frustration and hateful feelings she was having about her body and her life. She wrote them all down in a list. It was a long list.

Then Evy did three things. First, she started a new list of things she liked about herself. She began with her hair and her hands, because she'd always been proud of them. But this list of good qualities did not come as quickly as the other list. She decided to sit in front of the mirror without any clothes on every day, three times a day, to work on this new list. She would set a little timer for 20 minutes to make herself stay there, because it was hard. All these negative thoughts and feelings were intense, and at times overwhelming. But before she would leave, she would find at least one new thing to like about her body or her life that she could add to the good list.

The second thing she did was to accept the negative feelings as her own. She took responsibility for them. She owned them. Then she did something else, a little practice she developed. She would say, "God, these are my feelings and thoughts. I accept them as mine. But I don't know what to do with them. You take them." So every day she would accept her feelings as her own, and then give them away to God.

Thirdly, she decided to forgive anyone and everyone she needed to forgive. She did this daily.

Over time, Evy's list of positive qualities grew longer, and eventually it became as long as the old list. Still, she kept practicing. Her new list began to grow much longer than the old list.

At some point, she literally crossed a threshold. She wheeled into the mirror room and for the first time, all the negative thoughts and feelings had disappeared. They simply weren't there anymore. All she could feel for herself that day was love and compassion. Not only for her body, which she now saw as a miracle of creation and a vehicle that still served her, but also for the person, the soul that she was inside. She was able to see herself as a blessed being who could experience these wonderful feelings and thoughts, and as a person who had done much good in the world.

Still, she kept practicing.

At some point, she began to have more strength in her limbs. Pretty soon after that, she could walk again, feed herself, clothe herself, and do everything normally. Evy became the first person to completely recover from A.L.S. When that happened, she realized she must have more work to do in the world.

After listening to her story, I realized my problem with depression could be from a similar origin: not enough self-appreciation and esteem. I decided to write a song about her, which I did, and to do everything I could to make my life about love.

A few months later, I was back in Kansas City recovering from a ruptured spleen. I was still in a deep depression, and had been referred to a doctor for counseling, an old acquaintance named Bowen White. I had a couple of sessions with Bowen and he helped me a lot. In addition, Bowen is the kind of doctor who becomes your friend as well as your doctor, and his friendship was of great comfort to me.

One night, another friend called to tell me Bowen was giving a talk for the local cancer support group, and asked if I wanted to go hear him speak. I had no idea Bowen ever gave talks, so I said sure. I was intrigued.

It's hard to describe what happened that night. Bowen was one of the best speakers I'd ever heard. He had great rapport, a tremendous sense of humor, and fantastic material. Strangely, as I listened to him I kept noticing places in his talk where songs of mine would fit perfectly, like they were written for it.

To my astonishment, near the end of his talk, Bowen told the story of Evy McDonald and how she had healed herself through love and forgiveness. I was stunned at this synchronicity.

The next day I called Bowen and told him he needed to hear some of my songs. We got together, I played him the songs that I "heard" during his talk, including Evy's song, and he was as amazed as I had been. We immediately started teaming up to inflict ourselves on unsuspecting groups when our individual schedules permitted, something we have continued to do to this day with great delight.

But this wasn't all. It turned out Bowen knew Evy personally, and through him I was able to contact her. I sent her the song I had written about her, and she wrote back a lovely note telling me how she and all her friends had cried when they heard it. Some months later I was traveling in her vicinity and got to spend a day with her. I experienced first hand what a great soul she is. I noticed how all day long she gave her best stuff away to everybody, indiscriminately.

Evy made a couple of points clear to me during our visit. She emphasized that this "miracle" she experienced was not the miracle she was going for. She'd had a fatal illness. She'd expected to die.

All she was trying to do was have some love and compassion for herself before that happened. If she could just get to a place where she accepted and loved herself unconditionally before she died, then that would be enough for this lifetime.

Secondly, her whole life had been about service. She was a nurse, as I mentioned, and before that she'd been a candy striper who broke the record for hours volunteered in her local hospital. But when she got sick, she realized all her service had been what she called either Type I or Type II service. That is, service done either for reward and recognition, or service done out of a sense of duty. Evy wondered if there could be a third type: service done purely from love. And she decided that from this point on all her service would be about love. Even if she was sick.

As of this writing, in 2006, Evy has been totally recovered from Lou Gehrig's disease for 26 years. She has recently gone back to school and changed careers to become a minister. She has her own congregation, loves her "work," and is as happy as ever. She's discovered that service done purely from love is as beneficial for the giver as the receiver. She gets filled up on the outflow.

As for me, my depression lifted and hasn't come back for 15 years.

Evy has asked me to let people know that she feels she has already shared everything she can about her experience, and has recorded these thoughts for people who are interested in learning more. Rather than try to contact her, she requests that you obtain the recordings from newroadmapfoundation.org

Bowen White has written some wonderful books, including the excellent "Why Normal Isn't Healthy." He can be reached at www.bowenwhite.com

UNCONDITIONAL LOVE
The True Story of Evy McDonald
(Greg Tamblyn)

Evy had a body like a bowl of jello in a wheelchair
Evy had a nerve disease, all she could do was sit there
Evy was wasting away, muscles all in decay
She heard the doctor say, six months to live

Evy'd always said she hated her body,
she was overweight
And now a disease was making her thin,
what a twist of fate
She was almost out of time,
but somewhere in her mind
There was something she had to
find out if she could give

She said it's something called unconditional love
Supposed to be really wonderful stuff
And if you can get enough,
you can find peace
So in the time that I've got left
I've got to find some for myself
I believe unconditional love is what I need

Since all Evy could do was just
sit in the wheelchair
Evy rolled it over and sat there
in front of the mirror
She looked at her body and caught,
every negative thought
And though there were a lot,
she wrote 'em all down

Now every day Evy would sit there naked
at the mirror and look
Till she found one good thing about herself
to write in her book

And after a few months time,
her thoughts began to grow kind
And the negative words in her mind
could not be found

She said it feels like unconditional love
And it's really wonderful stuff
And if you can get enough,
you can find peace
So in the time that I've got left
I've got to find some for myself
I believe unconditional love is what I need

But a funny thing happened when Evy
started learning to love herself
The deterioration just stopped,
then reversed itself
And Evy was moving her arms and legs,
and starting to feel
Yes a funny thing happened,
Evy started to heal

First chorus

*"Draw a crazy picture... Write a nutty poem
Sing a mumble-gumble song... Whistle through your comb
Do a loony-goony dance 'Cross the kitchen floor
Put something silly in the world ...That ain't been there
before. " ~ Shel Silverstein*

Chapter 22

If Hollywood made a movie of your life starring Robin Williams, would you change? Patch Adams hasn't.

Spending a day with Patch made me feel like I've been looking at the world with blinders on. He is so original, so unique, that just hanging out with him forced me immediately reevaluate my own life from a new perspective.

Patch may be the most intentional person I've ever met or even read about.

Patch dresses like a clown every day. He's 6 feet 6 inches or something and hard to ignore. He claims to be able to take over any room of people and make it fun. He goes to Russia every year with 20 or so people (anybody can go) and clowns for kids in hospitals. He sleeps 3-5 hours a night. He's read the collected works of every important author you can name, fiction or non. He loves dancing and kissing. He doesn't own anything. He's interested in community, not capitalism. He answers his own phone. He answers his own letters, in longhand. He loves chaos.

He used to call wrong numbers for an hour a day just to practice talking to people. He wants to get to know you. He wants to serve you. He is not afraid to confront you. Although he wants to know your story, he doesn't want to wallow in it, or hear you use it as an excuse. He wants to know what you want. Right now. If you need love, he will love you. If you need to be held for hours, he will do that. If you want fun, you'll have fun. Friendship is his religion. Service is his God. Fun is his method.

He ran a free hospital *in his home* for 12 years. His interviews with patients take five hours. He has never charged for a service. No fees, no third party payments. He is now raising money for his new totally free hospital, The Geshundheit Institute, which is the first silly hospital in the world.

Robin Williams was paid 19 million dollars to play Patch, who as I mentioned has never charged a fee for medical services. The irony of this is not lost on Patch. It cost four times the price of the hospital to make the movie. It cost 1.5 times the price of the hospital to market the movie.

Patch feels the world is wallowing in misery. He believes that one of the most radical things you can do, and one of the absolute best ways you can serve the world, is to have a good day. And show it! Figure out a way to enjoy yourself, and let people know that it's a good thing and a fun thing because you're making it that way.

Patch is a great listener, and he's a great talker, which is a rare combination. I asked him how he dealt with people who are boring. He said he tells them, lovingly, that they are boring him. I asked him if he was always an extrovert, he said always. Even as a nerdy kid. And he was a nerd. But when he got old enough and made the decision to live the way he does, he gave himself exercises to do — like going into a bar and not leaving till he'd heard everyone's story. He wanted to learn how to relate to people. He needed to know how to engage anybody in conversation. He has made himself into who he is — who he wanted to be. He is never sick, never has a bad day. He is constantly and consistently outrageous.

He suggested I carry my guitar with me everywhere for a month and see what happened. See how people related to me. Play songs every chance I got. See how the conversations went. See how I related to people. Inject some surprise, some fun, some bizarreness into their day and mine.

I think it's a good idea. A bit troublesome, maybe, but worth it. Do I have the guts and persistence to do it? I don't know. But what a great experiment.

Bernie Siegel, by the way, says you don't have to dress like a clown or have a gimmick — just look at the world through the eyes of a child. See how absurd it is, and comment on it.

But I also think it's good to dress up and be a clown sometimes. We need to practice being outrageous. Great freedom comes in taking the risk. I learned this in my twenties delivering singing telegrams. I remember singing a telegram one night at the baseball stadium dressed like Tarzan, wearing only a loincloth in front of literally thousands of people. After that I felt like I could do anything.

Patch is somebody it's good to come into contact with. He reminds me that I'm living in other people's ruts sometimes. That I do a lot of things without thinking about them. Or because I think I have to. Or that I don't do a lot of things because I think I can't. And that as much fun as I have, I don't spend enough time being outrageous. Not enough time each day in the "absurd zone," where the world looks crazy and I see it for what it is.

By the way, Patch doesn't care if anybody laughs when he clowns. He's not doing it for you. It's for him. And thus for you, if you get it. And this is an important point. You have to have a little bit of that "don't give a shit" attitude. Life is crazy, life is bizarre. You might as well enjoy it and have some fun. And be true to you. Serve mankind by having a great day and letting people know it.

Since you might not get the opportunity to be around Patch right away, I suggest reading his short book, *Geshundheit!* It will make you think differently.

"You can discover more about a person in an hour of play than in a year of discussion." ~ Plato

Chapter 23

DAD FINALLY GETS AN ACE

My dad passed away in February. We had him cremated and gave him a loving, upbeat service telling stories and singing songs. But as it turned out, we weren't finished. The way we finally sent him off was a little different.

His 80th birthday would have been July 2. So all of us in the family converged at my brother's house for dinner. We ate, talked, and played games until around 10 pm, when it became completely dark outside. Then all 15 of us, from my little grade-schooler nephews to my 80 year old mother, siblings and in-laws, dressed up in our darkest burglar clothes, and sneaked onto the golf course where Dad had been a member for 40 years.

While a couple hundred people were doing their social thing a stone's throw away in the clubhouse, we creeped around in the dark and spread handfuls of Dad's ashes on some of the holes we knew he liked. We also put some in the lake, where our giant mutant labrador used to submerge himself in the reeking mud, then romp around the course mounting unsuspecting golfers who were bending over their bags at exactly the wrong time. (Dad always offered to pay for their dry cleaning.)

We finished up in a circle on the 18th fairway, singing Happy Birthday to him as loud as we could, then ran back to our cars before they could catch us and kick us off the course.

What I loved about this whole goofy goodbye ritual is how into it we all were. Even the littlest kids were grabbing handfuls of Dad and gently lofting him into the breeze. It was a great family outing. A real team-building experience. But what I liked most was Mom's idea to put some ashes in the cup of Dad's favorite par 3, so he could finally get a hole in one!

Very cool, Mom.

SO LONG, DAD
(Greg Tamblyn)

So long, Dad, it's time to leave your
body and move on
Another chapter in your education
And even though I'm feeling so sad
that you have gone
I hope for you this feels like graduation

They tell me that you travel through
a tunnel full of light
Hopefully that's fun and not confusing
And if it's true you do a big review of
your whole life
I hope for your sake God finds it amusing

So long, you're leavin' with our love
Though your body's gone,
you're not forgotten
Go on, to some better place above
If I do something good,
I hope you're watchin'

Think of all the mysteries you'll
finally get to know
Will the universe keep growing or
start shrinking?
Is there heaven? Is there hell?
And how 'bout UFOs?
And what the heck are women
really thinking?

If you meet your ancestors, t
here'll be much to say
You and all your relatives relating

Since bodies here on earth need
chromosomes and DNA
Please thank them all for me
for procreating

I hope there's peace and happiness
for everyone who dies
God knows you had your share of
life's frustrations
You never had a hole in one or won
a Nobel prize
But maybe you could try
reincarnation

So long, you're leavin' with our love
I know you realize how very much
Go on, to some better place above
And if it's possible,
please keep in touch.

So long, Dad

GREG TAMBLYN, NCW*
*(No Credentials Whatsoever)

Greg Tamblyn wanted to be a rock star from an early age, so he majored in....Geology! He followed that with graduate work in Planetarium Science, then detoured through careers in sales and marketing before becoming a professional songwriter and performer. He now specializes in opening and closing conferences with humorous musical keynote presentations for groups that want to laugh, lighten up, look at life differently, and live more effectively. His goal is to help people see the best in themselves, and laugh at the rest of themselves. When not roaming the planet, he lives in Kansas City, with access to eight nieces and nephews as well as several dogs.

Greg's CDs, DVDs, and booking information can befound at his website:

www.gregtamblyn.com

CPSIA information can be obtained at www.ICGtesting.com
Printed in the USA
LVOW060957041011

248977LV00001B/1/A